All About **OSHA**

U.S. Department of Labor

Occupational Safety and Health Administration

OSHA 3302-06N
2006

Contents

OSHA's Mission . . . 3

Introduction . . . 4

OSHA Coverage . . . 6

State Programs . . . 8

Standards & Guidance . . . 9

The Standards-Setting Process . . . 10

Reporting . . . 13

OSHA Enforcement Activities . . . 15

Enhanced Enforcement Program . . . 16

The OSHA Whistleblower Program . . . 16

Filing a Complaint . . . 17

Outreach, Education and Training, and Compliance Assistance . . . 18

OSHA's Cooperative Programs . . . 22

Business Feedback . . . 29

OSHA National Office Directorates . . . back cover

OSHA's Mission

Employers are responsible for providing a safe and healthful workplace for their employees. OSHA's role is to assure the safety and health of America's workers by setting and enforcing standards; providing training, outreach, and education; establishing partnerships; and encouraging continual process improvement in workplace safety and health.

OSHA establishes and enforces protective standards and reaches out to employers and employees through technical assistance and consultation programs. OSHA and its state partners have approximately 2,400 inspectors and about 550 state consultants, plus complaint discrimination investigators, engineers, physicians, educators, standard writers, and other technical and support personnel spread over more than 130 offices throughout the country.

OSHA works to assure the safety and health of all of America's working men and women. Most employees in the nation come under OSHA's jurisdiction. Other users and recipients of OSHA services include: occupational safety and health professionals, the academic community, lawyers, journalists, and personnel of other government entities.

Part of OSHA's mission is to provide assistance to employers to reduce or eliminate workplace hazards. OSHA provides a vast array of informational and training materials focusing on numerous safety and health hazards in the workplace.

For more information, visit OSHA's website at www.osha.gov.

OSHA stands ready to help both employers and employees in ensuring a safe and healthy workplace.

Introduction

The *Occupational Safety and Health Act of 1970* created the Occupational Safety and Health Administration to help employers and employees reduce injuries, illnesses and deaths on the job in America. Since then, workplace fatalities have been cut by more than 60 percent and occupational injury and illness rates have declined 40 percent. At the same time, U.S. employment has more than doubled and now includes over 115 million workers at 7.2 million worksites.

OSHA provides national leadership in occupational safety and health. The agency seeks to find and share the most effective ways to help prevent worker fatalities, and prevent workplace injuries and illnesses.

When employees stay whole and healthy, businesses also benefit. They experience lower workers' compensation insurance costs, reduced medical expenditures, decreased payout for return-to-work programs, fewer faulty products, and lower costs for job accommodations for injured workers. There are also indirect benefits such as increased productivity, lower costs for training replacement workers and decreased costs for overtime.

OSHA's impact

Since OSHA's creation in 1970, the nation has made substantial progress in occupational safety and health. OSHA and its many partners in the public and private sectors have for example:

- Cut the work-related fatality rate to historic lows for 2002 to 2004;
- From 2003 to 2004, reduced the number of workplace injuries and illnesses by 4 percent and lost workday case rates dropped by 5.8 percent in that same period;

- Virtually eliminated brown lung disease in the textile industry;
- In 2005, OSHA conducted close to 39,000 inspections and issued just over 85,000 citations for violations;
- In 2004, the Consultation Program made over 31,000 visits to employers.

OSHA's continuing role

Significant hazards and unsafe conditions still exist in U.S. workplaces. Each year:

- Almost 5,200 Americans die from workplace injuries in the private sector;
- Perhaps as many as 50,000 employees die from illnesses in which workplace exposures were a contributing factor;
- Nearly 4.3 million people suffer non-fatal workplace injuries and illnesses; and
- The cost of occupational injuries and illnesses totals more than $156 billion.

What OSHA does

OSHA uses three basic strategies, authorized by the *Occupational Safety and Health Act*, to help employers and employees reduce injuries, illnesses, and deaths on the job:

- Strong, fair, and effective enforcement;
- Outreach, education, and compliance assistance; and
- Partnerships, Alliances and other cooperative and voluntary programs.

Based on these strategies, OSHA conducts a wide range of programs and activities to promote workplace safety and health. The agency:

- Encourages employers and employees to reduce workplace hazards and to implement new safety and health management systems or improve existing programs;
- Develops mandatory job safety and health standards and enforces them through worksite

inspections, and, sometimes, by imposing citations, penalties, or both;

- Promotes safe and healthful work environments through cooperative programs including the Voluntary Protection Programs, OSHA Strategic Partnerships, and Alliances;
- Establishes responsibilities and rights for employers and employees to achieve better safety and health conditions;
- Supports the development of innovative ways of dealing with workplace hazards;
- Establishes requirements for injury and illness recordkeeping by employers, and for employer monitoring of certain occupational illnesses;
- Establishes training programs to increase the competence of occupational safety and health personnel;
- Provides technical and compliance assistance, and training and education to help employers reduce worker accidents and injuries;
- Works in partnership with states that operate their own occupational safety and health programs; and
- Supports the Consultation Programs offered by all 50 states, the District of Columbia, Puerto Rico, the Virgin Islands, Guam and the Northern Mariana Islands.

OSHA Coverage

The OSH Act covers private sector employers and their employees in the 50 states and certain territories and jurisdictions under federal authority. Those jurisdictions include the District of Columbia, Puerto Rico, the Virgin Islands, American Samoa, Guam, Northern Mariana Islands, Wake Island, Johnston Island, and the Outer Continental Shelf Lands as defined in the *Outer Continental Shelf Lands Act*.

The OSH Act covers employers and employees either directly through Federal OSHA or through an OSHA-approved state program.

Who is not covered
The OSH Act does not cover:
- The self-employed;
- Members of immediate family of farm employers that do not employ outside workers;
- Worker conditions that are regulated under worker safety or health requirements of other federal agencies;
- Employees of state and local governments; some states have their own occupational safety and health plans that cover these workers.

Federal worker coverage
Section 19 of the OSH Act makes federal agency heads responsible for providing safe and healthful working conditions for their employees. OSHA conducts federal workplace inspections in response to employee reports of hazards.

The OSH Act also requires federal agencies to comply with standards consistent with those for private sector employers. Under a 1998 amendment to the Act, it covers the U.S. Postal Service the same as any private sector employer.

State and local government worker coverage
OSHA provisions cover the private sector only. However, some states have their own OSHA-approved occupational safety and health programs. These state programs cover state and local government employees.

State safety and health programs
State plans are OSHA-approved job safety and health programs operated by individual states instead of Federal OSHA. The OSH Act encourages states to develop and operate their own job safety and health plans and precludes state enforcement of OSHA standards unless the state has an approved plan. OSHA approves and monitors all state plans. The state plans must be at least as effective as Federal OSHA requirements.

State plans covering the private sector also must cover state and local government employees. OSHA rules also permit states and territories to develop plans that cover only public sector (state and local government) employees. In these cases, private sector employment remains under Federal OSHA jurisdiction. Twenty-two states and territories operate complete plans and four cover only the public sector. These states are listed below and on the OSHA website at www.osha.gov.

State program coverage
States with approved plans cover most private sector employees as well as state and local government workers in the state. Federal OSHA continues to cover federal employees and certain other employees specifically excluded from a state's plan; for example, in some states those who work in maritime industries and on military bases.

The following states have OSHA-approved State Plans:

- Alaska
- Arizona
- California
- Connecticut
- Hawaii
- Indiana
- Iowa
- Kentucky

- Maryland
- Michigan
- Minnesota
- Nevada
- New Jersey
- New Mexico
- New York
- North Carolina
- Oregon
- Puerto Rico
- South Carolina
- Tennessee
- Utah
- Vermont
- Virgin Islands
- Virginia
- Washington
- Wyoming

NOTE: The Connecticut, New Jersey, New York and Virgin Islands plans cover public sector (state and local government) employment only.

Standards & Guidance

Requirements

In general, OSHA standards require that employers:

- Maintain conditions or adopt practices reasonably necessary and appropriate to protect workers on the job;
- Be familiar with and comply with standards applicable to their establishments; and
- Ensure that employees have and use personal protective equipment when required for safety and health.

Hazards addressed

OSHA issues standards for a wide variety of workplace hazards, including:

- Toxic substances;
- Harmful physical agents;
- Electrical hazards;
- Fall hazards;
- Trenching hazards;
- Hazardous waste;
- Infectious diseases;

- Fire and explosion hazards;
- Dangerous atmospheres;
- Machine hazards; and
- Confined spaces.

In addition, where there are no specific OSHA standards, employers must comply with the OSH Act's "general duty clause." The general duty clause, Section 5(a)(1), requires that each employer "furnish ... a place of employment which [is] free from recognized hazards that are causing or are likely to cause death or serious physical harm to his employees."

The Standards-Setting Process

Deciding to develop a standard

OSHA can begin standards-setting procedures on its own initiative or in response to petitions from other parties, including:
- The Secretary of Health and Human Services (HHS);
- The National Institute for Occupational Safety and Health (NIOSH);
- State and local governments;
- Nationally recognized standards-producing organizations and employer or labor representatives; and
- Any other interested parties.

Each spring and fall, the Department of Labor publishes in the Federal Register a list of all regulations that have work underway. The Regulatory Agenda provides a schedule for the development of standards and regulations so that employers, employees, and other interested parties can know when they are expected.

How OSHA develops standards

OSHA publishes its intention to propose, amend, or revoke a standard in the Federal Register, either as:

- A Request for Information or an Advance Notice of Proposed Rulemaking or announcement of a meeting to solicit information to be used in drafting a proposal; or
- A Notice of Proposed Rulemaking, which sets out the proposed new rule's requirements and provides a specific time for the public to respond.

These actions are posted online at www.regulations.gov. Interested parties may submit written information, comments and evidence. In addition, OSHA may also schedule a public hearing to consider various points of view.

After reviewing public comments, evidence and testimony, OSHA publishes:

- The full text of any standard amended or adopted and the date it becomes effective, along with an explanation of the standard and the reasons for implementing it; or
- A determination that no standard or amendment is necessary.

Input from other government agencies

Other government agencies can recommend standards to OSHA. The OSH Act established the National Institute for Occupational Safety and Health in the Department of HHS as the research agency for occupational safety and health. NIOSH conducts research on various safety and health problems, provides technical assistance to OSHA, and recommends standards for OSHA's consideration. (For more information, call (800) 35-NIOSH or visit the agency's website at www.cdc.gov/ niosh).

Input from small business

The Small Business Regulatory Enforcement Fairness Act of 1996 (SBREFA), gives small businesses help in understanding and complying with OSHA regulations and allows them to have more of a voice in developing new regulations. Under SBREFA, OSHA must:

- Produce Small Entity Compliance Guides for some agency rules;
- Be responsive to small business inquiries about complying with the agency's regulations;
- Have a penalty reduction policy for small businesses;
- Involve small businesses in developing proposed rules expected to significantly affect a large number of small entities through Small Business Advocacy Review Panels; and
- Give small businesses the opportunity to challenge in court agency rules or regulations that they believe will adversely affect them.

For more information, visit OSHA's website at www.osha.gov/dcsp/smallbusiness/sbrefa.html.

Advisory Groups

OSHA has several standing advisory committees and *ad hoc* advisory committees that advise the agency on safety and health issues. These committees include representatives of management, labor, and state agencies as well as one or more designees of the Secretary of Health and Human Services (HHS). Members also may include representatives of occupational safety and health professions and the general public.

The two standing, or statutory, advisory committees are:
- The National Advisory Committee on Occupational Safety and Health (NACOSH),

which advises, consults with, and makes rec-
ommendations to the U.S. Secretaries of Labor
and HHS on matters regarding administration
of the OSH Act; and
* The Advisory Committee on Construction
Safety and Health (ACCSH), which advises the
Secretary of Labor on construction safety and
health standards and other matters.

Other continuing advisory committees include:
* The Federal Advisory Council on Occupational
Safety and Health (FACOSH), which advises
the Secretary of Labor on all aspects of federal
agency safety and health; and
* The Maritime Advisory Committee for
Occupational Safety and Health (MACOSH),
which advises the Secretary of Labor on workplace safety and health programs, policies and
standards in the maritime industry.

OSHA may occasionally form short-term advisory
committees to advise the agency on specific issues.

Guidelines versus standards
A guideline is a tool to assist employers in recognizing and controlling hazards. It is voluntary and
not enforceable under the OSH Act. Failure to
implement a guideline is not itself a violation of
the OSH Act's general duty clause.

Guidelines can be developed quickly and can be
changed easily as new information becomes
available with scientific advances. Guidelines
make it easy for employers to adopt innovative
programs to suit their workplaces.

Reporting

OSHA's reporting requirements
All employers must report to OSHA within eight
hours of learning about:

- The death of any employee from a work-related incident; and
- The in-patient hospitalization of three or more employees as a result of a work-related incident.

In addition, employers must report all fatal heart attacks that occur at work. Deaths from motor vehicle accidents on public streets (except those in a construction work zone) and in accidents on commercial airplanes, trains, subways or buses do not need to be reported.

These reports may be made by telephone or in person to the nearest OSHA area office listed at www.osha.gov or by calling OSHA's toll-free number, (800) 321-OSHA (6742).

Employers may be subject to other reporting requirements in other OSHA standards as well.

OSHA's recordkeeping requirements

The *Occupational Safety and Health Act of 1970* (OSH Act) requires covered employers to prepare and maintain records of occupational injuries and illnesses. OSHA is responsible for administering the recordkeeping system established by the Act. The OSH Act and recordkeeping regulations provide specific recording and reporting requirements which comprise the framework for the nationwide occupational safety and health recording system.

Under this system, it is essential that data recorded by employers be uniform and accurate to assure the consistency and validity of the statistical data which is used by OSHA for many purposes, including inspection targeting, performance measurement, standards development, resource allocation, Voluntary Protection Program (VPP) and Safety and Health Recognition Program (SHARP) eligibility, and "low-hazard" industry exemptions. The data will also aid employers, employees, compliance officers and consultants in analyzing the safety and health environment at the employer's establishment.

OSHA Enforcement Activities

Carrying out our mission

Enforcement plays an important part in OSHA's efforts to reduce workplace injuries, illnesses, and fatalities. Through OSHA's Site-Specific Targeting and Enhanced Enforcement programs, the agency sends a clear message that it takes its mission seriously. When the agency finds employers who fail to uphold their employee safety and health responsibilities, OSHA deals with them strongly.

In addition, OSHA administers and supports a comprehensive field occupational safety and health guidance and compliance assistance effort within a variety of industry sectors including general industry, maritime, construction, and health. OSHA also administers and evaluates occupational safety and health programs for all federal agencies, assisting them in providing safe and healthful working conditions for their employees.

OSHA also sets rules for the Federal Advisory Council on Occupational Safety and Health, administers an anti-discrimination program to protect the rights of employees to seek safe and healthful working conditions, and operates the cargo gear accreditation program for certifying vessels' cargo gear and shore-based material handling devices.

OSHA carries out its enforcement activities through its 10 regional offices and 90 area offices. OSHA's regional offices are located in Boston, New York City, Philadelphia, Atlanta, Chicago, Dallas, Kansas City, Denver, San Francisco and Seattle.

Enhanced Enforcement Program (EEP)

- OSHA's Enhanced Enforcement Program targets employers who have a history of the most severe safety and health violations.
- This approach helps OSHA focus on employers who willfully and repeatedly expose their employees to the most serious hazards, refuse to correct violations and violate their safety and health agreements.
- The EEP's concentration on high gravity violators strengthens the agency's enforcement program and enhances the focus on corporate-wide offenders.

The OSHA Whistleblower Program

To help ensure that employees are free to participate in safety and health activities, Section 11(c) of the OSH Act prohibits any person from discharging or in any manner retaliating or discriminating against any employee because the employee has exercised rights under the Act. These rights include complaining to OSHA and seeking an OSHA inspection, participating in an OSHA inspection, and participating or testifying in any proceeding related to an OSHA inspection.

"Discrimination" can include the following actions:
- Firing or laying off
- Blacklisting
- Demoting
- Denying overtime or promotion
- Disciplining
- Denial of benefits
- Failure to hire or rehire
- Intimidation
- Reassignment affecting promotion prospects
- Reducing pay or hours

To file a complaint under Section 11(c), contact the nearest OSHA office within 30 days of the discrimination. Discrimination complaints cannot be filed online.

OSHA also administers the whistleblowing provisions of thirteen other laws protecting employees from retaliation for reporting violations of various trucking, airline, nuclear, pipeline, environmental, and corporate fraud and securities laws. Each statute has its own deadline and form of filing. For details, see www.osha.gov/dep/oia/whistleblower or contact OSHA.

Filing a Complaint

Hazardous workplace complaints
If your workplace has unsafe or unhealthful working conditions, you may want to file a complaint. Often the best and fastest way to get it corrected is to notify your supervisor or employer.

Employees also may file a complaint by phone, mail, e-mail, or fax with the nearest OSHA office and request an inspection. You may also ask OSHA not to reveal your name. To file a complaint, call (800) 321-OSHA (6742) or contact the nearest OSHA regional, area, state plan, or consultation office listed at www.osha.gov. The teletypewriter (TTY) number is (877) 889-5627.

You can also file a complaint online. Most online complaints may be resolved informally over the phone with your employer. Written, signed complaints submitted to OSHA area or state plan offices are more likely to result in onsite OSHA inspections. Complaints from employees in states with an OSHA-approved state plan will be forwarded to the appropriate state plan for response. If you are concerned about confidentiality, you should file your complaint from either your home computer or one in your local library.

Download the OSHA complaint form, complete it, and then fax or mail it to your local OSHA office or simply contact your local OSHA office to receive a copy of the complaint form. Include your name, address, and telephone number so that we can contact you. (NOTE: To view and print the OSHA complaint form, you must have the Adobe Acrobat Reader on your computer.)

Discrimination complaints
If you believe that your employer has discriminated against you because you exercised your safety and health rights, contact your local OSHA office right away. Most discrimination complaints fall under the OSH Act, which gives you only 30 days to report discrimination. Some of the other laws have complaint-filing deadlines that differ from OSHA's, so be sure to check. For complete information visit www.osha.gov.

Outreach, Education and Training, and Compliance Assistance

Outreach materials on OSHA's website
OSHA's website provides extensive information about the agency as well as standards, interpretations, directives, technical advisors, compliance assistance, and additional information. The site also includes electronic assistance tools, such as eTools and interactive Expert Advisors, information on specific health and safety topics, videos, and other information for employers and employees. The OSHA website's address is www.osha.gov.

In addition, OSHA's website includes several special features:

- Spanish-language pages that provide workplace safety and health information in Spanish;
- A Small Business page, designed to increase awareness among small business owners about their responsibilities under the OSH Act, and resources to help them at www.osha.gov/smallbusiness.
- A Compliance Assistance page that provides a portal to OSHA's compliance assistance resources and information on OSHA's cooperative programs.
- A Workers page that explains employees' rights and responsibilities under the OSH Act.
- A Teen Workers page that addresses safety and health issues for employees under the age of 18.
- An OSHA Training Institute Education Centers page that provides information such as course listings, events, FAQs and a list of all the Education Centers in each OSHA region.

These and other web-based resources are available at www.osha.gov.

OSHA Training and Education
OSHA's Training Institute in Arlington Heights, IL,
provides basic and advanced courses in safety
and health for federal and state compliance officers, state consultants, federal agency personnel
and private sector employers, employees and
their representatives.

The OSHA Training Institute also has established
OSHA Training Institute Education Centers (not
funded by OSHA) to address the increased
demand for its courses from the private sector
and from other federal agencies. These centers
are nonprofit colleges, universities and other
organizations that have been selected after a com-
petition for participation in the program.

The education centers help administer OSHA's
Outreach Training Program — the agency's pri-
mary way to train workers in the basics of occupational safety and health. Those who complete a
one-week OSHA training course are authorized to
teach 10-hour or 30-hour courses in construction

or general industry safety and health standards. These individuals go on to train thousands more students each year.

OSHA also provides funds to nonprofit organizations, through grants, to conduct workplace training and education in subjects where OSHA believes there is a lack of workplace training. Grants are awarded annually. Grant recipients are expected to contribute 20 percent of the total grant cost.

For more information on grants, training and education, contact the OSHA Training Institute, Office of Training and Education, 2020 South Arlington Heights Road, Arlington Heights, IL 60005, (847) 297-4810 or see "Training" on OSHA's website at www.osha.gov.

Compliance assistance materials

OSHA's Compliance Assistance Specialists provide general information about OSHA standards and compliance assistance resources. They respond to requests for help from a variety of groups, including small businesses, trade associations, union locals and community and faith-based groups. There is one Compliance Assistance Specialist in each OSHA Area Office in states under federal jurisdiction.

OSHA publications

OSHA has an extensive publications program. The agency publishes booklets, fact sheets and cards detailing various facets of OSHA policy and regulations.

Many publications are now available in Spanish as well as English to ensure that Spanish-speaking employees also have access to important workplace safety and health information.

All OSHA publications can be downloaded at no cost from the agency's website at www.osha.gov. In addition, most are available in hardcopy form, some at no cost from OSHA and others for purchase from the U.S. Government Printing Office. For a list of available publications, visit www.osha.gov, call (800) 321-OSHA (6742), or fax to (202) 693-2498.

OSHA's Cooperative Programs

Voluntary, cooperative relationships among employers, employees, unions, and OSHA can be a useful alternative to traditional OSHA enforcement and an effective way to reduce employee deaths, injuries, and illnesses. OSHA has several types of cooperative programs:
- Alliance Program
- Consultation Program and the Safety and Health Achievement Recognition Program (SHARP)
- OSHA Strategic Partnerships
- Voluntary Protection Programs

Alliance Program
OSHA's Alliance Program, established in 2002, enables organizations committed to workplace safety and health to collaborate with OSHA to prevent injuries and illnesses in the workplace. OSHA and its allies work together to reach out to, educate, and lead the nation's employers and their employees in improving and advancing workplace safety and health.

Benefits of participating
There are many benefits to participating in an Alliance with OSHA. Through this program, organizations will:
- Build trusting, cooperative relationships with the agency;

- Network with others committed to workplace safety and health;
- Access resources to maximize employee safety and health protection; and
- Gain recognition as a proactive leader in safety and health.

Eligible groups

Alliances are open to a variety of groups, including:
- Trade or professional organizations;
- Businesses;
- Labor organizations;
- Educational institutions; and
- Government agencies.

In some cases, organizations may be cooperating with OSHA for the first time. In others, they may be building on existing relationships with the agency that were developed through other cooperative programs such as strategic partnerships, the Voluntary Protection Programs, and consultation.

How Alliances work

Alliance agreements do not include an enforcement component, such as an exemption from general scheduled inspections or monitoring visits. Alliances are also different from other cooperative programs because their agreements are not worksite-based; instead they focus on entire industries or hazards within industries. However, OSHA and the participating organizations must define, implement, and meet a set of short- and long-term goals that fall into three categories:
- Training and education;
- Outreach and communication;
- Promoting the national dialogue on workplace safety and health.

After an Alliance is signed

OSHA and the program participants will form an implementation team. The team, consisting of OSHA and the organization's representatives, will develop strategies and begin implementing programs or processes for meeting the defined goals.

For more information about national Alliances, contact OSHA's Office of Outreach Services and Alliances at (202) 693-2340 or visit www.osha.gov/ alliances. For information about regional or local Alliances, contact the appropriate regional office listed on the website at: www.osha.gov, or call (800) 321-OSHA (6742).

OSHA Consultation Service

OSHA's Consultation Service is a free service that enables employers to identify potential hazards at their worksites and ways to correct them, improve their occupational safety and health management systems, and even qualify for a one-year exemption from routine OSHA inspection. The service is delivered by state governments using well-trained professional staff. Most consultations take place on-site, though limited services away from the worksite are available.

OSHA's Consultation Service provides on-site assistance in developing and implementing effective workplace safety and health programs that emphasize preventing employee injuries and illnesses. OSHA's comprehensive consultation assistance includes an appraisal of:
- Mechanical systems, physical work practices, and environmental hazards of the workplace; and
- Aspects of the employer's present job safety and health program. Employers also may receive training and education services as well as limited assistance away from the worksite.

Consultation assistance is available to smaller employers (with fewer than 250 employees at a fixed site and no more than 500 employees nationwide). Consultation programs are funded largely by OSHA and run by state agencies at no cost to the employer who requests help. OSHA does not propose penalties or issue citations for hazards identified by the consultant. The employer must correct all serious hazards and potential safety and health violations which the consultant identifies. However, if an employer does not correct violations identified through consultation assistance, the consultant may refer the employer for a possible inspection. The employer's name and firm as well as any information about the workplace will not be routinely reported to OSHA enforcement staff.

SHARP

By working with the OSHA Consultation Program, certain exemplary employers may request participation in OSHA's Safety and Health Achievement Recognition Program (SHARP). To be eligible for

SHARP participation, employers must receive a comprehensive consultation visit, have injury and illness rates below the industry average, demonstrate exemplary achievements in workplace safety and health by abating all identified hazards, and develop and implement an excellent safety and health program.

Employers accepted into SHARP may receive an exemption from OSHA programmed inspections— but not from OSHA investigations of complaints or accidents—for one year.

For more information about consultation assistance in your state, visit www.osha.gov/SHARP.

OSHA Strategic Partnership Program (OSPP)
OSHA Strategic Partnerships are voluntary, written, long-term agreements to form cooperative relationships between OSHA and groups of employers, employees, employees' union representatives, and sometimes other stakeholders (for example, trade and professional associations, universities and other government agencies). OSPs aim to have a measurable, positive impact on the American workplace by encouraging, assisting, and recognizing partners' efforts to eliminate serious hazards and to achieve a high level of employee safety and health.

These partnerships help participants:
- Establish effective safety and health management systems;
- Train managers and employees to recognize, and then eliminate or control, hazards common to their industry and their particular worksite;
- Give employees the opportunity to become involved meaningfully in their own protection; and
- Create ways for partners to share expertise and other resources.

How partnerships improve worker safety and health

Many OSHA Strategic Partnerships are designed to lead to the development and implementation of comprehensive workplace safety and health management systems. OSHA has found that a systems approach is the best strategy for reducing deaths, injuries and illnesses on the job. Other partnerships focus on the elimination or control of a specific industry hazard.

Benefits of participating

Participating in an OSHA Strategic Partnership offers such benefits as:

- Declines in workplace injuries and illnesses, and consequent reductions in workers' compensation and other injury- and illness-related costs;
- Improved employee motivation to work safely, leading to better quality and productivity;
- Development or improvement of safety and health management systems;
- Positive community recognition and interaction; and
- Partnership with OSHA.

Voluntary Protection Programs

Voluntary Protection Programs (VPP) represent one part of OSHA's effort to extend employee protection beyond the minimum required by OSHA standards. There are three VPP programs: Star, Merit, and Star Demonstration. OSHA designed them to:

- Recognize outstanding achievement of employers and employees who are working together to provide high-quality worker protection by implementing effective safety and health management systems;
- Motivate other employers to achieve excellent safety and health results in the same outstanding way; and

- Establish a cooperative relationship between employers, employees, and OSHA.

How VPP can help employers and employees
VPP participation can mean:
- Improved employee motivation to work safely, leading to better quality and productivity;
- Lost workday case rates generally 50 percent below industry averages;
- Reduced workers' compensation and other injury- and illness-related costs;
- Positive community recognition and interaction;
- Further improvement and revitalization of already good safety and health management systems; and
- Partnership with OSHA.

How OSHA monitors VPP sites
OSHA reviews an employer's VPP application and conducts an onsite review to verify that the safety and health systems described are operating effectively at the site. OSHA continues to conduct regular evaluations of approved sites.

All participants must submit to their OSHA regional office in February of each year a copy of the most recent annual evaluation conducted at the site. This evaluation must include the injury and illness numbers and rates for the past year.

OSHA inspections at VPP and SHARP sites
Sites participating in VPP and SHARP are exempt from programmed inspections. OSHA does respond, however, to employee complaints, serious accidents, or significant chemical releases that may occur according to routine enforcement procedures.

Employers and employees are recognizing that OSHA has changed and that the agency wants to work cooperatively with them to help improve their workplaces.

"We can't make a quality product with an unsafe process." – **Ken Lindgren, DACO, Inc.**

"It makes sense to run an effective safety and health program because your people deserve it, your customers demand it, and your business practices and future will not be there without it."
– **Dan Fergus, Genesee Stampings**

"Safety is a pass/fail item, in that if you fail at safety, the other stuff doesn't matter." – **Mac Armstrong, Air Transport Association**

"I want to see and hear my grandchildren, and because of the safety program at Curtis Lumber, I'm going to be able to." – **John Meier, Curtis Lumber**

"We feel that it is our duty to have every employee return home to his or her family sound and healthy every day." – **John Obel, NexTech**

"The health and safety of our people has always been of paramount importance to us. Our goal of zero incidents required teamwork like OSHA's Strategic Partnership Program, combined with relentlessly pursuing the elimination of unsafe actions and conditions." – **Walter Berry, Bollinger Shipyards, Inc.**

Additional small business success stories may be found on the OSHA small business web page at: www.osha.gov/smallbusiness.

**For further information
call (800) 321-OSHA or visit www.osha.gov**

OSHA National Office Directorates

Directorate of Construction
The Directorate of Construction develops workplace safety standards, guidance and outreach to ensure safe working conditions for the nation's construction workers. (202) 693-2020.

Directorate of Cooperative and State Programs
The Directorate of Cooperative and State Programs coordinates OSHA's role in carrying out training and education for employers and employees, implementing consultation and cooperative programs, and coordinating the agency's compliance assistance and outreach activities, as well as the agency's relations with state plan states. (202) 693-2200.

Directorate of Enforcement Programs
The Directorate of Enforcement Programs provides a balanced program for OSHA by establishing and maintaining a comprehensive occupational safety and health compliance guidance and assistance program and coordinating OSHA's inspection and enforcement programs. (202) 693-2100.

Directorate of Evaluation and Analysis
The Directorate of Evaluation and Analysis provides agency-wide evaluation and analytic leadership and services in support of OSHA program, legislative, regulatory, statistical, and policy development activities. (202) 693-2400.

Directorate of Science, Technology and Medicine
The Directorate of Science, Technology and Medicine supports other OSHA staff by providing specialized technical expertise and advice. (202) 693-2300.

Directorate of Standards and Guidance
The Directorate of Standards and Guidance contributes to ensuring safe and healthful working conditions in covered workplaces through development of workplace standards, regulations and guidance. (202) 693-1950.

The Office of Communications
The Office of Communications is responsible for media inquiries and publications development. (202) 693-1999.